Writer's Notebook

GRADE 2

Printed in the U.S.A.

ISBN   978-1-328-47010-2

9 10 11 12 13   0304   26 25 24 23 22

4500849058   A B C D E F G

Grade 2 Contents

MODULE 1: Personal Narrative

Develop a Research Plan 1.1

Word Bank 1.2

Ways Kids Make the World a Better Place 1.3

Set Goals for Writing 1.4

Develop an Idea for Your Narrative 1.5

Organize your Personal Narrative 1.6

Personal Narrative Model 1.7

Conferencing 1.10

Proofreading 1.11

Publishing Ideas 1.12

Revisit Your Writing Goals 1.13

Share Your Writing 1.14

MODULE 2: Descriptive Essay

Word Bank 2.1

Nouns and Adjectives 2.2

Getting Started 2.3

Set Goals for Writing 2.4

Insider Chart 2.5

Descriptive Essay Model 2.6

Organize Your Descriptive Essay 2.8

Draft Your Essay 2.9

Conferencing 2.10

Proofreading **2.11**

Publishing Ideas **2.12**

Revisit Your Writing Goals **2.13**

MODULE 3: Persuasive Text

Word Bank **3.1**

Choosing a Topic **3.2**

My Research Plan **3.3**

Set Goals for Writing **3.4**

Persuasive Text Model **3.5**

Research Notes **3.7**

Verb Tenses **3.8**

Conferencing **3.9**

Adverbs **3.10**

Proofreading **3.11**

Revisit Your Writing Goals **3.12**

MODULE 4: Imaginative Story

Word Bank **4.1**

Set Goals for Writing **4.2**

Get Started! **4.3**

Organizing My Story **4.4**

Imaginative Story Model **4.5**

My Lead Sentence **4.8**

Conferencing **4.9**

Proofreading **4.10**

My Publishing Idea 4.11
Revisit Your Writing Goals 4.12

MODULE 5: Personal Essay

Understanding Idioms................................ 5.1
Problem Solving 5.2
Word Bank.. 5.3
My Heart Map 5.4
Set Goals for Writing 5.5
Insider Chart 5.6
Personal Essay Model................................. 5.7
Conferencing... 5.9
Proofreading 5.10
Publishing My Personal Essay 5.11
Revisit Your Writing Goals 5.12
Share Your Writing 5.13

MODULE 6: Poem

Word Bank.. 6.1
Set Goals for Writing 6.2
Writing a Poem.. 6.3
Poem Model.. 6.4
Sensory Details Chart................................. 6.5
Conferencing... 6.6
Proofreading 6.7
Revisit Your Writing Goals 6.8
Share Your Writing 6.9

MODULE 7: Imaginative Story

Meet a Pirate!...........................7.1

My Word Bank..........................7.2

Set Goals for Writing................7.3

Character Traits.......................7.4

Imaginative Story Model...........7.5

Organize Your Story Ideas.........7.10

Problems and Solutions.............7.11

Dialogue Adds to a Story...........7.12

Conferencing............................7.13

Proofreading............................7.14

Published!................................7.15

Revisit Your Writing Goals.........7.16

Share Your Writing...................7.17

MODULE 8: Procedural Text

Conduct a Survey.....................8.1

Following Steps........................8.2

Word Bank...............................8.3

Questions about My Topic.........8.4

Set Goals for Writing................8.5

Steps for My Activity.................8.6

Procedural Text Model..............8.7

Conferencing............................8.9

Proofreading............................8.10

Are You Ready to Publish?.........8.11

Published! My How-To Paragraph...8.12

Published! My How-To List 8.13

Revisit Your Writing Goals 8.14

MODULE 9: Research Report

Cite Sources: An Example 9.1

Fact Sheet 9.2

Word Bank 9.3

My Research Plan 9.4

Animal Relationships 9.5

My Idea Map 9.6

Set Goals for Writing 9.7

My Research Notes 9.8

Research Report Model 9.9

My Report—Getting Started 9.11

Conferencing 9.12

Proofreading 9.13

Published! 9.14

Revisit Your Writing Goals 9.15

MODULE 10: Thank-You Letter

Word Bank 10.1

Culture Web 10.2

My Traditions and Cultural Experiences 10.3

Set Goals for Writing 10.4

Thank-You Letter Model 10.5

Parts of a Thank-You Letter 10.7

Conferencing 10.8

Pronouns 10.9
Proofreading 10.10
Revisit Your Writing Goals 10.11
Share Your Writing 10.12

MODULE 11: Personal Narrative

Class Poll 11.1
Word Bank 11.2
Set Goals for Writing 11.3
Ask Questions 11.4
Personal Narrative Model 11.5
Story Structure 11.9
Conferencing 11.10
Proofreading 11.11
Revisit Your Writing Goals 11.12

MODULE 12: Opinion Essay

My Dot 12.1
Word Bank 12.2
Opinion Essay Model 12.3
Set Goals for Writing 12.6
Support Your Opinion 12.7
Conferencing 12.8
Proofreading 12.9
Revisit Your Writing Goals 12.10

Name _____

Develop a Research Plan

Identify topic: What topic did the author of *Just a Dream* explore?

_____

_____

Ask a question: Write a research question on that topic.

_____

_____

Identify sources: What sources do you need to answer your research question?

_____

_____

_____

Gather sources: Where can you find those sources?

_____

_____

What do you think? How does developing and following a research plan help an author write a book?

_____

_____

Name _____

Word Bank

Write descriptive language from *Just a Dream*. You can use this Word Bank when you draft and revise your own personal narrative.

Use one or two words from the box in a sentence.

_____

_____

Name _____

Ways Kids Make the World a Better Place

Make notes in the chart below about ways kids help their friends, family, and community. Remember that a **community** is a group of people to which you belong, such as your school or your neighborhood.

Helping Friends	Helping Family	Helping the Community

Name _____

Set Goals for Writing

You are going to write a personal narrative. A personal narrative tells a story from the author's point of view.

1. Be sure your personal narrative includes:

   • a story that tells how you made the world a better place

   • a beginning, a middle, and an end

   • specific details

   • relevant details

   • correct spelling, capitalization, and punctuation

2. Be sure you follow each step of the writing process.

Write your own goals.

Goal 1: _____

Goal 2: _____

Why are these your goals?

Goal 1: _____

Goal 2: _____

Name _____

Develop an Idea for Your Narrative

Choose an idea for your personal narrative. Then ask yourself the questions in the chart below and record your answers. Be sure to provide specific and relevant details.

My Idea: _____

What did you do to make the world a better place?	
Where did this happen?	
When did this happen?	
Why did this happen?	

Name _____

Organize Your Personal Narrative

You will write a personal narrative. The main character is YOU. Think about your story idea. Then answer the questions in the chart below.

Beginning	What do you want the reader to know about you? _____ _____
Middle	Add specific and relevant details. Who did you help? _____ How did you help? _____ Where did you help? _____ Why did you help? _____
End	How did your action make the world a better place? _____ _____

Name _____

Personal Narrative

Title: <u>A Good Deed on a Snowy Day</u>

    It was a cold and wintry day. Usually, my brother Caden and I would have school. But not today! We had a snow day.

    Dad did not have a snow day. He still had to go to work. "I'll probably be home late," he said with a sigh. "Travel will be slow with all the snow."

Personal Narrative (continued)

The snow came down thicker and faster. Caden and I went outside and threw snowballs. We made a fort. We had fun!

We saw our neighbors coming home from work. They were tired, and they still had to shovel their sidewalks.

Caden and I thought of Dad. He would be tired, too. We decided to help! We shoveled our sidewalk and Mrs. Henshaw's walk next door.

$\rightarrow$

Name _____

Personal Narrative (continued)

"Look at what you've done!"
Dad said, smiling brightly as he
arrived home. "You two make
me proud." That made my heart
swell with happiness. I knew Mrs.
Henshaw would be glad and
surprised, too.

Caden and I agreed: having a
snow day is fun. It is great to play
in the snow. But the best part of
this day was helping others!

_____

_____

_____

_____

Name _____

Conferencing

Based on your classmates' feedback, circle **YES** if the answer to the question is yes. Circle **NO** if you still need to work on that element.

Does my narrative need more information? If yes, add words, phrases, or sentences to explain ideas better.	YES NO
Does my narrative have information that does not support the central idea? If yes, delete words, phrases, or sentences that do not belong.	YES NO
Are my ideas clear? If no, rearrange words, phrases, or sentences so your readers can understand what you are saying.	YES NO
Did I use the pronoun I? Did I capitalize it? If no, revise so that the narrative is told using the pronoun I.	YES NO
Did I explain how one small action made the world better? If no, add details that are specific and relevant.	YES NO

How will you fix it?

Pick one item in your writing that you want to improve. Explain how you will improve it.

Name _____

Proofreading

Proofreading a Personal Narrative Written by

_____

Editors Write your name next to the item you are checking.
Circle **YES** if the answer is yes. Circle **NO** if the answer is no.

Editor's Name	Question		
	Does the paper have the writer's name?	YES	NO
	Are possessives spelled correctly?	YES	NO
	Are contractions spelled correctly?	YES	NO
	Are prepositional phrases used correctly?	YES	NO
	Does each sentence start with a capital letter?	YES	NO
	Does each sentence end with correct punctuation?	YES	NO
	Is the pronoun "I" capitalized?	YES	NO

Writers Use this feedback to edit your draft for the items in the list.

Name _____

Publishing Ideas

List your publishing ideas. Put a check mark next to the idea you like best.

1. _____

2. _____

3. _____

Tell why you like the checked idea best for your personal narrative.

Name _____

Revisit Your Writing Goals

How Did I Do? Congratulations! You finished your personal narrative. Look at the goals you set on Writer's Notebook page 1.4 or in your notebook. Did you meet them? What could you do better with your next piece of writing? Write two or three sentences that tell how you think you did.

_____

_____

_____

_____

_____

_____

_____

_____

_____

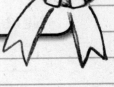

Name _____

Share Your Writing

Make a check mark in the box if the answer is yes. When I shared my personal narrative orally, did I:

- [ ] read in a loud, clear voice?
- [ ] read with expression?
- [ ] group phrases for meaning?
- [ ] use punctuation to know when to pause?
- [ ] use punctuation to know when to ask a question?
- [ ] use punctuation to know when to use emotion?
- [ ] look at the audience?

How Did I Do? Think about how you shared your personal narrative. Complete the sentence frames below.

When I shared my personal narrative, I liked _____

_____ .

Next time I share my writing, I would like to _____

_____ .

Name _____

Word Bank

Add words that describe. Refer to these words when you begin drafting your descriptive essay.

Name _____

Nouns and Adjectives

Add words to the chart.

Nouns	Adjectives

Use words from the chart. Pick a noun with your partner. Write a sentence using that noun and an adjective from your chart.

_____

_____

Draw your sentence. Discuss with your partner.

Name _____

Getting Started

Use this chart to help you choose a place.

Places I'd like to visit:

Put a star next to one place in the box above.
Write questions about that place in this box.

Sources I might use to answer those questions:

Name _____

Set Goals for Writing

You are going to write a descriptive essay. A descriptive essay gives facts and details about a topic. It includes an introduction, a body, and a conclusion.

1. Be sure your descriptive essay includes:

   • a clear lead sentence about your topic in the introduction

   • details that develop the topic in the body

   • a strong conclusion that wraps up the topic

   • correct spelling, capitalization, and punctuation

2. Be sure you follow each step of the writing process.

Write your goals.

Goal 1: _____

Goal 2: _____

Why are these your goals?

Goal 1: _____

Goal 2: _____

Name _____

Insider Chart

You will write an essay describing a place you would like to visit. Organize your information for your essay in the chart below.

Place I'd Like to Visit	Insider Information	Source

Name _____

Descriptive Essay

Title: <u>Mexico City</u>

    Do you know Mexico City? I don't, but I want to.

    I hear there are colorful birds and colorful clothes to see. Even the parks are colorful. There are flowers that are red, yellow, pink, and more. If it rains, I can go to a museum. The museum tells stories about the people of Mexico City. After all this sightseeing, I will be hungry.

→

Name _____

Descriptive Essay (continued)

     Did you know there are people selling food from carts in Mexico City? They sell the food right on the street! I might get a spicy taco, or a hot chorizo with eggs, or a churro. I can almost smell the spices, especially the cinnamon. This is making me hungry!

     Mexico City sounds fun. I hope I get to visit Mexico City someday. Don't you?

_____

_____

_____

_____

Name _____

Organize Your Descriptive Essay

Use your notes and Insider Chart information. Complete the sections below.

Introduction: State the topic

Body: Provide details

Conclusion: Retell the main idea

Name _____

Draft Your Essay

Demonstrate understanding of the information you have gathered by writing a draft of your descriptive essay below. Use information from Writer's Notebook page 2.8 or your notes. Remember to include an introduction, the body, and a conclusion.

My title: _____

My name: _____

_____

_____

_____

_____

_____

_____

_____

_____

_____

Name _____

Conferencing

Based on your classmates' feedback, circle **YES** if the answer to the question is yes. Circle **NO** if you still need to work on that element.

Do I need more information? If yes, add words, phrases, or sentences to explain ideas better.	YES NO
Do I have information that does not support the central idea? If yes, delete words, phrases, or sentences that are not needed.	YES NO
Are my ideas clear? If no, rearrange words, phrases, and sentences so your readers can understand what you are saying.	YES NO
Does my essay have an introduction, a body, and a conclusion? If no, use your planning and drafting notes to help organize the ideas.	YES NO
Does the lead sentence make me interested in the topic?	YES NO

How will you fix it?

Pick one item in your writing that you want to improve. Explain how you will improve it.

_____

Proofreading

Proofreading a Descriptive Essay Written by

_____

Editors Write your name next to the item you are checking.
Circle **YES** if the answer is yes. Circle **NO** if the answer is no.

Editor's Name	Question		
	Does the paper have the writer's name?	YES	NO
	Does the first word of each sentence begin with a capital letter?	YES	NO
	Does each sentence have a noun and a verb?	YES	NO
	Does each sentence end with proper punctuation?	YES	NO
	Are all words spelled correctly?	YES	NO

Writers Use this feedback to edit your draft for the items in the list.

Name _____

Publishing Ideas

List your publishing ideas. Put a check mark next to the idea you like best.

1. _____

2. _____

3. _____

What will your published writing look like? Draw your idea in the box.

Name _____

Revisit Your Writing Goals

How Did I Do? Think about your writing goals. Place a check mark in the column that shows how you did.

Did I meet this goal?	Yes	No	Almost
I wrote a clear lead sentence about my topic in the introduction.			
The body had details that told more about my topic.			
The conclusion summarized my topic.			
I used correct spelling, capitalization, and punctuation.			
My Goal:			
My Goal:			

Name _____

Word Bank

Add words that describe emotions. Refer to these words when you begin drafting your persuasive text.

Name _____

Choosing a Topic

Answer each question by circling the choice that best fits your opinion on the topic.

School days should be longer.	YES	NO	NO OPINION
Cats make the best pets.	YES	NO	NO OPINION
We should wear school uniforms.	YES	NO	NO OPINION

What other topics do you have an opinion about? List your ideas.

1. _____

2. _____

3. _____

Read your ideas. Identify a topic you have a strong opinion about.

My topic is _____

My opinion is _____

_____

Name _____

My Research Plan

1. Identify my topic.

My topic is _____

2. State my opinion.

My opinion is _____

3. Write questions to help find facts to support my opinion.

Question 1: _____

_____

Question 2: _____

_____

Question 3: _____

_____

4. List sources to use to find facts.

_____

_____

_____

_____

Name _____

Set Goals for Writing

You are going to write a persuasive text. A persuasive text uses facts and examples to persuade a reader's opinion on a topic.

1. Be sure your persuasive text includes:

    • a clear opinion statement

    • details such as facts, statements, and examples that are specific and relevant to your opinion

    • adverbs that answer the questions *when*, *how*, and *where*

    • prepositional phrases

    • a strong conclusion that sums up the writer's point of view

2. Be sure you follow each step of the writing process.

Write your own goals.

Goal 1: _____

Goal 2: _____

Why are these your goals?

Goal 1: _____

Goal 2: _____

Name _____

Persuasive Text

Title: <u>Why Dogs Are the Best Pets</u>

Do you have a pet? I have a dog. I believe that dogs are the best pets.

Dogs can help people stay active. Many people have fun walking their dogs. Playing fetch with a dog can often bring people joy. Being outside getting exercise is wonderful for both dogs and humans!

Dogs are usually very smart animals. Dogs can learn many tricks. They can also be trained to carefully obey their owners.

Persuasive Text (continued)

Dogs are very loyal pets. Dogs are bundles of excitement every time they see you! Nothing says "welcome home" like the happily wagging tail of a pet dog!

Dogs bring happiness everywhere they go. This is why dogs make the best pets.

Sources

Clarke, D.J. Why Dogs Make Good Pets. 2015.

Ing, Sean. Train Your Dog. 2018.

Research Notes

Use this page to help you make notes about the information you find in your research.

My question: _____

_____

Fact from book: _____

_____

_____

Fact, in my words: _____

_____

_____

_____

My source: Primary | Secondary

Title: _____

Author: _____

Date: _____

Citation: _____

Verb Tenses

Check your draft for verbs. Write each verb from your draft in the correct column.

Present	Past	Future
Example: walk	Example: walked	Example: will walk

Are all your verbs in the same column? _____

If no, do you need to revise your draft? _____

If yes, how will you revise it? _____

Name _____

Conferencing

Based on your classmates' feedback, circle **YES** if the answer to the question is yes. Circle **NO** if you still need to work on that element.

Do I need more information? If yes, add words, phrases, or sentences to explain ideas better.	**YES** **NO**
Do I have information that does not support your opinion? If yes, delete words, phrases, or sentences that are not needed.	**YES** **NO**
Are my ideas clear? If no, rearrange words, phrases, and sentences so your readers can understand what you are saying.	**YES** **NO**
Does the lead sentence state my opinion clearly? If no, fix it.	**YES** **NO**
Do I have three facts that are specific and relevant? If no, add them.	**YES** **NO**

How will you fix it?

Pick one item in your writing that you want to improve. Explain how you will improve it.

_____

_____

Name _____

Adverbs

Check your draft for adverbs. Write each adverb from your draft in the correct column. Underline each preposition in the adverb phrase answering the question *Where?*

When	How	Where
Example: **after** dinner	Example: ran **quickly**	Example: **by the tree**

Do your adverbs make your text more clear? _____

If not, what can you do to fix it? _____

Now, reread your draft. Add more adverbs as needed to help make your persuasive text stronger.

Proofreading

Proofreading a Persuasive Text Written by

_____

Editors Write your name next to the item you are checking.

Circle **YES** if the answer is yes. Circle **NO** if the answer is no.

Editor's Name	Question		
	Does the paper have the writer's name?	YES	NO
	Is the correct verb tense (present, past, or future) used throughout the writing?	YES	NO
	Does the writing use adverbs that answer the question "When?"	YES	NO
	Does the writing use adverbs that answer the question "Where?"	YES	NO
	Does the writing use prepositions in prepositional phrases?	YES	NO

Writers Use this feedback to edit your draft for the items in the list.

Name _____

Revisit Your Writing Goals

How Did I Do? Think about your persuasive text. Place a check mark next to each goal you met.

- [ ] I included a clear opinion statement.

- [ ] I included details such as facts, statements, and examples that are specific and relevant to my opinion.

- [ ] I included adverbs that answer the questions *when*, *how*, and *where*.

- [ ] I used prepositional phrases.

- [ ] I included a strong conclusion that sums up my point of view.

Did you meet other goals? Add them here.

- [ ] _____

- [ ] _____

Name _____

Word Bank

Add words you can use.

Name _____

Set Goals for Writing

You are going to write an imaginative story based on an imaginary place or character. It will include a beginning, a middle, and an end.

1. Be sure your imaginative story includes:

- an interesting beginning

- at least one character based on your imagination

- a middle that states a problem

- a solution to the problem

- a strong ending

2. Be sure you follow each step of the writing process.

Write your goals.

Goal 1: _____

Goal 2: _____

Why are these your goals?

Goal 1: _____

Goal 2: _____

Be sure to use this checklist as you brainstorm ideas for your imaginative story and as you draft it.

Name _____

Get Started!

Write and draw about ideas for imaginary friends and places.

Brainstorm	
Imaginary Friends	**Imaginary Places**
_____ _____ _____ _____	_____ _____ _____ _____
Draw	**Draw**
Write _____ _____	**Write** _____ _____

Name _____

Organizing My Story

Write what your story is about and where it takes place.

My imaginary story is about

_____

My imaginary story takes place

_____

More about my story

Beginning	Middle	End

Imaginative Story

Title: The Glowing Mountain

"Wow! Look at that huge glowing mountain!" Manny points and shouts.

"Hey, wait up," calls his sister, Susanna. Then she stops in her tracks. "I've never seen anything so amazing," she whispers.

"Let's get closer," Manny continues. "Look, the glow from the mountain is everywhere. It's as if everything is on fire!"

The bright light beckons them closer. Manny and Susanna climb up the steep path.

Name _____

Imaginative Story (continued)

    At first, Manny and Susanna enjoy exploring. But then Susanna hears a monstrous noise.

    "Manny," she hisses, "make your stomach stop that awful growling!"

    "That's not my stomach," he grunts. "I thought that terrible sound was coming from you."

    Suddenly afraid, the children start running as quickly as their feet will carry them. But soon, they stop in their tracks. The mountain's glow surrounds them, locking them tightly in a prison-like cell.

$\rightarrow$

Imaginative Story (continued)

"We're trapped," Manny yells. Slowly, a teardrop falls onto Susanna's cheek. Then another tear and another fall. All at once, she is crying so hard that buckets of water fall from the sky. Manny starts to cry too. Their tears soak the ground around them.

Suddenly, everything turns dark. The mountain's fiery glow is gone, and the children are free. They race away and don't stop until they reach home.

Name _____

My Lead Sentence

Write Your Lead

Remember, your lead should grab the reader's attention. Write a lead for your story on the lines below.

_____

_____

_____

Write the Feedback

Write what your partner says about your lead.

_____

_____

Rewrite Your Lead

Now, rewrite your lead. Remember, you can add, delete, or rearrange details to make your lead more interesting.

_____

_____

_____

Name _____

Conferencing

Based on your classmates' feedback, circle **YES** if the answer to the question is yes. Circle **NO** if you still need to work on that element.

Do I need more information? If yes, add words, phrases, or sentences to explain ideas better.	**YES** **NO**
Do I have information that does not support the central idea? If yes, delete words, phrases, or sentences that are not needed.	**YES** **NO**
Are my ideas clear? If no, rearrange words, phrases, and sentences so your readers can understand what you are saying.	**YES** **NO**
Does the lead sentence make me interested in the topic?	**YES** **NO**
Are the problem and solution clear?	**YES** **NO**

How will you fix it?

Pick one item in your writing that you want to improve. Explain how you will improve it. _____

_____

_____

Proofreading

Proofreading an Imaginative Story Written by

_____

Editors Circle **YES** if the answer is yes. Circle **NO** if the answer is no.

This story was checked by _____

Question		
Does the paper have the writer's name?	YES	NO
Does each sentence begin with a capital letter?	YES	NO
Do all proper nouns begin with a capital letter?	YES	NO
Does each subject agree with its verb?	YES	NO
Does each sentence end with proper punctuation?	YES	NO
Are all words spelled correctly?	YES	NO

Writers Use this feedback to edit your draft for the items in the list.

Name _____

My Publishing Idea

Write an idea for a cover. Then draw a cover for your story.

My story is about

_____

My cover might show

_____

Name _____

Revisit Your Writing Goals

How Did I Do? Think about your imaginative story.

Did you meet your goals? Place a check mark next to each goal you met.

- [ ] I *used* ideas from my imagination.
- [ ] I included a lead in the *beginning*, a *middle*, and an *end*.
- [ ] I *used* descriptive words.
- [ ] I included a *problem* and a *solution*.
- [ ] I *edited* my writing for errors in capitalization and punctuation.
- [ ] I *edited* my writing for errors in spelling.

Did you meet other goals? Add them here.

- [ ] _____
- [ ] _____

Name _____

Understanding Idioms

Draw and write about a time when you had to stand tall.
How did it make you feel?

_____

_____

Problem Solving

Name one problem Molly Lou solved.
Draw about it.

Write about it.

_____

_____

Name _____

Word Bank

Write adjectives in the box.

Write a simile and a metaphor.

Simile: _____

Metaphor: _____

My Heart Map

Draw a big heart. What makes you special?
Write your ideas in the heart.

Name _____

Set Goals for Writing

1. Be sure your personal essay includes:

   • a lead sentence that tells about you

   • details and examples to support the main idea

   • similes or metaphors that paint a picture about you

   • transition words that show how details are related to the topic and each other

   • a strong conclusion that sums up the information

2. Be sure you follow each step of the writing process.

Write your goals.

Goal 1: _____

Goal 2: _____

Why are these your goals?

Goal 1: _____

Goal 2: _____

Use these goals to help you write your personal essay.

Name _____

Insider Chart

Explain what makes you unique. Organize your information in the chart below.

Ways We Differ	Insider Information	Central Idea

Name _____

Personal Essay

Title: <u>I Am Unique</u>

    What people notice first about me is that I am tall. In fact, I am very tall.

    People think that because I am tall I am good at playing basketball. They are wrong! Once, I tried to dribble the ball while I was running. I fell down. I felt as clumsy as an ox!

$\rightarrow$

Name _____

Personal Essay (continued)

It is OK that I am not good at basketball. I found something I am very good at. I am good at gymnastics. I have good balance and I can reach the high bar without any help. Walking on the balance beam makes me feel as graceful as a swan.

I used to think it was hard being tall. But I have finally learned that being tall is part of what makes me special.

_____

_____

_____

_____

Name _____

Conferencing

Based on your classmates' feedback, circle **YES** if the answer to the question is yes. Circle **NO** if you still need to work on that element.

Does my *essay* have an introduction with a lead sentence, a body, and a conclusion? If no, use your planning and drafting notes to help organize the ideas.	**YES NO**
Do I have information that does not support the central idea? If yes, delete words, phrases, or sentences that are not needed.	**YES NO**
Are my ideas clear? If no, rearrange words, phrases, and *sentences* so your readers can understand what you are saying.	**YES NO**
Do I need more information? If yes, add words, phrases, or sentences to explain ideas better using specific and relevant details.	**YES NO**
Did I use linking words to connect ideas? If no, look for places where you can add linking words.	**YES NO**

Put a star next to one or two items you want to focus on as you continue to revise your personal essay.

Name _____

Proofreading

Proofreading a Personal Essay Written by

_____

Editors Write your name next to the item you are checking.

Circle **YES** if the answer is yes. Circle **NO** if the answer is no.

Editor's Name	Question		
	Does the paper have the writer's name?	YES	NO
	Is the pronoun "I" capitalized?	YES	NO
	Are all proper nouns capitalized?	YES	NO
	Does each subject agree with its verb?	YES	NO
	Are all words spelled correctly?	YES	NO

Writers Use this feedback to edit your draft for the items in the list.

Publishing My Personal Essay

One idea: Draw a picture of a mirror. Write or tape your essay inside the mirror. Use this or your own idea to publish your personal essay in the space below.

Remember to write capital and lowercase letters of the alphabet. Sign the essay using your first and last names.

Revisit Your Writing Goals

How Did I Do? Think about your personal essay. Place a check mark next to each goal you met.

- [ ] I wrote a lead sentence that tells about me.
- [ ] I added details and examples to support the central idea.
- [ ] I used similes or metaphors that paint a picture about me.
- [ ] I used transition words that show how details are related to the topic and each other.
- [ ] I wrote a strong conclusion that sums up the information.
- [ ] I followed each step of the writing process.
- [ ] I edited my writing for errors in capitalization and punctuation.
- [ ] I edited my writing for errors in spelling.

Did you meet other goals? Add them here.

- [ ] _____
- [ ] _____

Name _____

Share Your Writing

When your partner shared the personal essay, did your partner:

☐	read in a loud, clear voice?
☐	read with expression?
☐	group phrases for meaning?
☐	use punctuation to know when to pause?
☐	use punctuation to know when to ask a question?
☐	use punctuation to know when to use emotion?
☐	look at the audience?

Mark a check in the box if the answer is yes. Give the paper to your partner.

Share with your partner. Use sentence frames to talk about how your partner shared.

When you shared your essay, you _____ .

I like how you _____ when you shared your essay.

Name _____

Word Bank

Add words that tell about weather.

Use two of the words to write sentences about weather. Underline each weather word.

_____

_____

Name _____

Set Goals for Writing

1. Be sure to do the following in your poem:

   • Write a title.

   • Write about weather, using short lines of text.

   • Write one or two stanzas.

   • Use rhyming words, if possible.

   • Use sensory words (words that will help the reader hear, see, taste, feel, or smell what you are describing).

   • Use correct spelling, capitalization, and punctuation.

2. Be sure you follow each step of the writing process.

Write your goals.

Goal 1: _____

Goal 2: _____

Why are these your goals?

Goal 1: _____

Goal 2: _____

Name _____

Writing a Poem

My topic is _____ .

My poem will be about _____ .

Words about my topic: _____

_____

_____

_____

Poem

Title: <u>My Kite in the Wind</u>

<u>The brisk wind hisses in my ear</u>
<u>Letting me know it is near.</u>
<u>I race the wind with my bright red kite</u>
<u>And, on the blustery wind's wings,</u>
<u>I stop and watch my kite take flight.</u>

<u>A fresh wind rushes for my kite</u>
<u>Lifting it almost out of sight.</u>
<u>Breezes blowing with a swoosh</u>
<u>And, on the blustery wind's wings,</u>
<u>I stand and watch my kite go whoosh.</u>

Name _____

Sensory Details Chart

Think about your audience. Add sensory details to help them see, hear, feel, taste, and smell details in your poem.

In my poem, the weather is _____ .

When I think about my poem, I might:

See	
Hear	
Feel	
Taste	
Smell	

Write a sentence using two of your sensory details.

_____

_____

Conferencing

Based on your classmates' feedback, circle **YES** if the answer to the question is yes. Circle **NO** if you still need to work on that element.

Do I need more information? If yes, add words, phrases, or sentences to explain ideas better.	YES NO
Do I have information that does not support the central idea? If yes, delete words, phrases, or sentences that are not needed.	YES NO
Are my ideas clear? If no, rearrange words, phrases, and sentences so my readers can understand what I am saying.	YES NO
Does my poem use sensory words that are specific and relevant to my topic?	YES NO
Does my poem use stanzas to organize my ideas?	YES NO

How will you fix it?

Pick one item in your writing that you want to improve. Explain how you will improve it.

_____

_____

Name _____

Proofreading

Proofreading a Poem Written by _____

Editors Write your name next to the item you are checking.
Circle **YES** if the answer is yes. Circle **NO** if the answer is no.

Editor's Name	Question		
	Is the writer's name on the paper?	YES	NO
	Are capital letters used correctly in the title?	YES	NO
	Does each line begin with a capital letter?	YES	NO
	Is the pronoun "I" capitalized?	YES	NO
	Does each sentence end with correct punctuation?	YES	NO
	Is there space between each stanza?	YES	NO
	Are words spelled correctly?	YES	NO

Writers Use this feedback to edit your draft.

Name _____

Revisit Your Writing Goals

How Did I Do? Think about your poem. Place a check mark next to each goal you met.

☐	I wrote a title.
☐	I wrote about weather in short lines of text.
☐	I wrote one or two stanzas.
☐	I used rhyming words.
☐	I used words to help the reader hear, see, taste, feel, or smell what I described.
☐	I edited my writing for errors in capitalization.
☐	I edited my writing for errors in spelling.

Did you meet other goals? Add them here.

☐ _____

☐ _____

Name _____

Share Your Writing

Mark a check in the box if the answer is yes.
When I read my poem orally, did I:

- ☐ read in a loud and clear voice?
- ☐ read with expression?
- ☐ group phrases for meaning?
- ☐ use punctuation to know when to pause?
- ☐ use punctuation to know when to ask a question?
- ☐ use punctuation to know when to use emotion?
- ☐ look at the audience?

How Did I Do? Think about how you shared your poem.

When I shared my poem, I liked _____

_____.

Next time I share my writing, I would like to _____

_____.

Name _____

Meet a Pirate!

Draw a pirate. Then use words to describe this character.

Name _____

My Word Bank

Add words you can use.

My Character

Write or draw about your character.

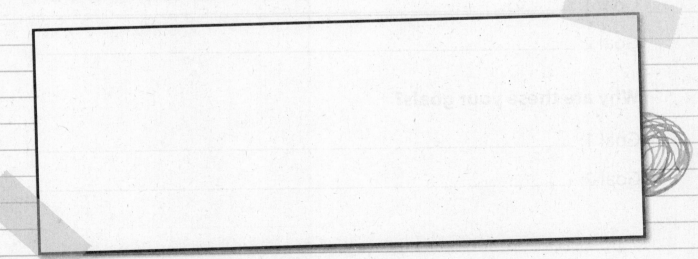

More About My Character

My character _____.

My character might say, "_____."

Name _____

Set Goals for Writing

1. Be sure your imaginative story includes:

   • a strong character

   • descriptive words and dialogue

   • a plot that includes a problem and a solution

   • a beginning that gives the background

   • a middle that gives specific and relevant details

   • an end that tells how the problem was solved

2. Be sure you follow each step of the writing process.

Write your goals.

Goal 1: _____

Goal 2: _____

Why are these your goals?

Goal 1: _____

Goal 2: _____

Character Traits

Write about your main character.

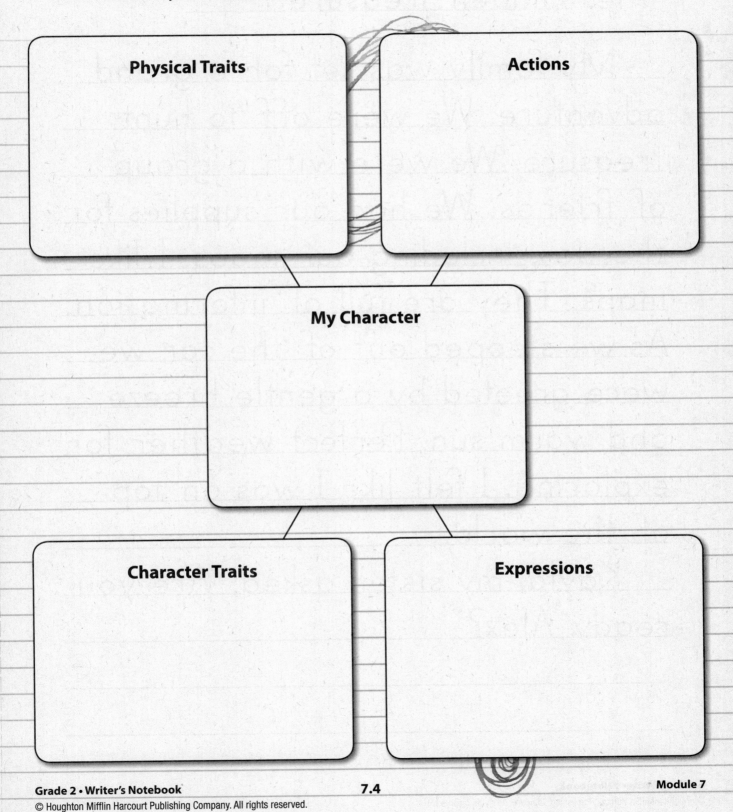

Physical Traits

Actions

My Character

Character Traits

Expressions

Name _____

Imaginative Story

Title: <u>Hidden Treasure</u>

   My family was set for a grand adventure. We were off to hunt treasure. We were with a group of friends. We had our supplies for the day, including our maps. I like maps. They are full of information. As we stepped out of the car, we were greeted by a gentle breeze and warm sun. Perfect weather for exploring. I felt like I was on top of the world.

   Kayla, my sister, asked, "Are you ready, Alex?"

Imaginative Story (continued)

"Yes! I have a copy of our map in my pocket. Finding this hidden treasure will be a piece of cake." Nothing would stop me now.

As we hiked, we sang silly songs. Then, the trail started to go uphill. We had to climb up and over huge boulders. I could not keep up with the others.

"I know a faster way to the top," I told my family. I pulled out the map. "We can take this path to get a little ahead of the others. That will give us a chance at finding the treasure first."

Imaginative Story (continued)

"Hold your horses," Kayla exclaimed. "I don't want to get lost."

"We won't," I said. I put the map away and took a quick drink from my water bottle.

I pointed to a narrow path in the grass off to the side. "If we go this way, we will still go up the hill without climbing all the rocks."

We caught up with the others in a few minutes. They were roaming around a wooded area. Everyone was looking for the hidden treasure.

Imaginative Story (continued)

Stepping behind a tree, I looked at my map. I had written clues before we left home. Now I could use my notes to find the hidden cache.

Without saying anything, I motioned to Kayla. She followed me as I snuck around a couple of large boulders. We waded through tall grass to get to a stand of trees. I started digging by an old, gnarly oak. Kayla looked at me and said, "I think you are barking up the wrong tree."

$\rightarrow$

Name _____

Imaginative Story (continued)

    I pointed to a drawing on the map. Kayla looked at the map. Then she pointed to a stone and said, "I think you want this jagged stone."

    We moved the stone. A small box lay half buried in the dirt. We pulled it out and started jumping up and down.

    "We found it!" we yelled. "We have the hidden treasure." Wow! What a day. Together, Kayla and I proved to be successful explorers.

Name _____

Organize Your Story Ideas

Write about your story ideas to organize your writing.

Beginning: Tell about your main character.

Middle: State the problem. Give specific and relevant details.

End: Solve the problem here.

Problems and Solutions

Think about the kinds of problems your character might face on his or her adventure. Fill in the chart.

Problems	Traits	Solutions

Pick one trait. How does it help solve the problem?

_____

_____

Name _____

Dialogue Adds to a Story

Draw your characters.

Give your characters speech bubbles. In the speech bubbles,
write what your characters say to each other.

Conferencing

Based on your classmates' feedback, circle **YES** if the answer to the question is yes. Circle **NO** if you still need to work on that element.

Do I need more information? If yes, add words, phrases, or sentences to better explain ideas using specific and relevant details.	**YES** **NO**
Do I have information that does not support the central idea? If yes, delete words, phrases, or sentences that are not needed.	**YES** **NO**
Are my ideas clear? If no, rearrange words, phrases, and sentences so your readers can understand what you are saying.	**YES** **NO**
Do I state and solve a problem? If no, add specific and relevant details about the problem and solution.	**YES** **NO**
Do I use dialogue effectively? If no, add, delete, or rearrange words to fix it.	**YES** **NO**

How will you fix it?

Pick one item in your writing that you want to improve. Explain how you will improve it. _____

_____

Proofreading

Proofreading an Imaginative Story Written by

_____

Editors Circle **YES** if the answer is yes. Circle **NO** if the answer is no.

This story was checked by _____

Question		
Does the paper have the writer's name?	YES	NO
Does each sentence start with a capital letter?	YES	NO
Does each sentence use end punctuation correctly?	YES	NO
Is there an opening quotation mark for dialogue?	YES	NO
Is there a closing quotation mark for dialogue?	YES	NO
Is a comma used to set off the person speaking?	YES	NO
Are all words spelled correctly?	YES	NO

Writers Use this feedback to edit your draft.

Published!

Draw a heart. Publish your story inside the heart.
Or, use your own publishing idea.

Name _____

Revisit Your Writing Goals

How Did I Do? Think about your imaginative story. Place a check mark next to each goal you met.

- [ ] I used descriptive words and dialogue.
- [ ] I wrote a plot that includes a problem and a solution.
- [ ] My story has a beginning that gives the background.
- [ ] My story has a middle that tells the main events.
- [ ] My story has an end that tells how the problem was solved.
- [ ] I followed the steps in the writing process.
- [ ] I edited my writing for errors in capitalization and punctuation.
- [ ] I edited my story for spelling errors.

Did you meet other goals? Add them here.

- [ ] _____
- [ ] _____

Share Your Writing

Mark a check in the box if the answer is yes.

When I read my imaginative story, did I:

- ☐ read in a loud, clear voice?
- ☐ read with expression?
- ☐ group phrases for meaning?
- ☐ use punctuation to know when to pause?
- ☐ use punctuation to know when to ask a question?
- ☐ use punctuation to know when to use emotion?
- ☐ look at the audience?

What did your classmates have to say?

When I shared my story, they said that I _____

_____ .

They liked how I _____

_____ when I shared my story.

Name _____

Conduct a Survey

Ask your classmates: What is your favorite season?

Write your classmates' initials in the proper column starting with the bottom box. Color the boxes with initials. Use a different color for each column.

Winter	Spring	Summer	Fall

Which season is the favorite based on your results?

_____

Congratulations! You gathered information using first-person accounts. You used primary sources.

Name _____

Following Steps

Think about what you learned in *From Seed to Plant*. What steps are needed to turn a seed into a plant? Write the steps in order in the boxes below.

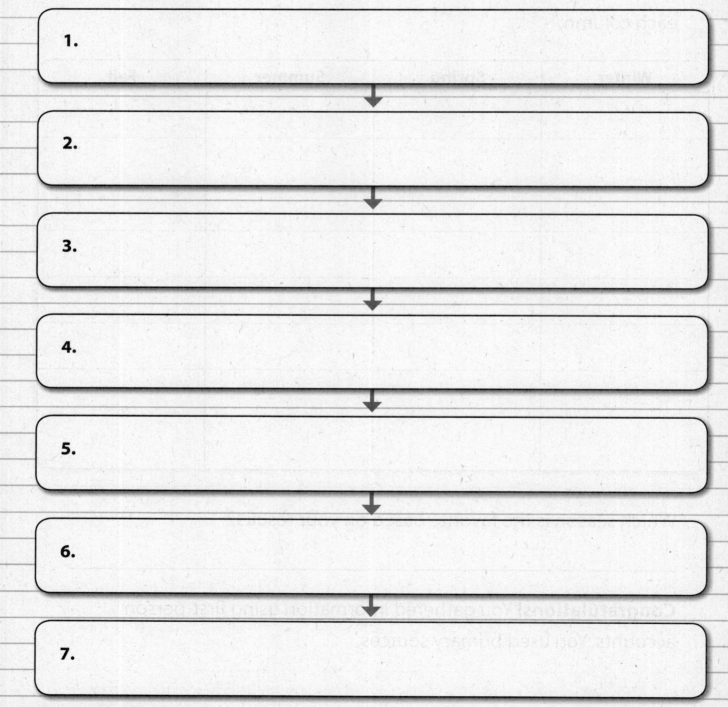

1.

2.

3.

4.

5.

6.

7.

Name _____

Word Bank

Add words that signal time order.

Refer to these words when you begin drafting your procedural text.

Write two sentences using words from the box. Write sentences that show time order. Underline the time-order words you used.

_____

_____

Name _____

Questions About My Topic

In your procedural text, you will write the steps to complete an activity that needs to be done in a set order. Write your ideas for topics in the box below. Then place a star by one idea you want to explore more.

Write formal questions about your starred topic.

_____

_____

Write informal questions about your starred topic.

_____

_____

Name _____

Set Goals for Writing

1. When writing your procedural text, be sure to:

- state your topic clearly

- ask formal and informal questions about your topic

- find primary and secondary sources to answer the questions

- use transition words to show time-order sequence

- use parallel structure when creating a list of steps

- use correct spelling, capitalization, punctuation, grammar, and sentences

2. Be sure you follow each step of the writing process.

Write your goals.

Goal 1: _____

Goal 2: _____

Why are these your goals?

Goal 1: _____

Goal 2: _____

Name _____

Steps for My Activity

My Topic: _____

Sketch Your Steps Draw a simple sketch in each box to remind you what needs to happen at that step. If you need more boxes, add them to a page in your notebook.

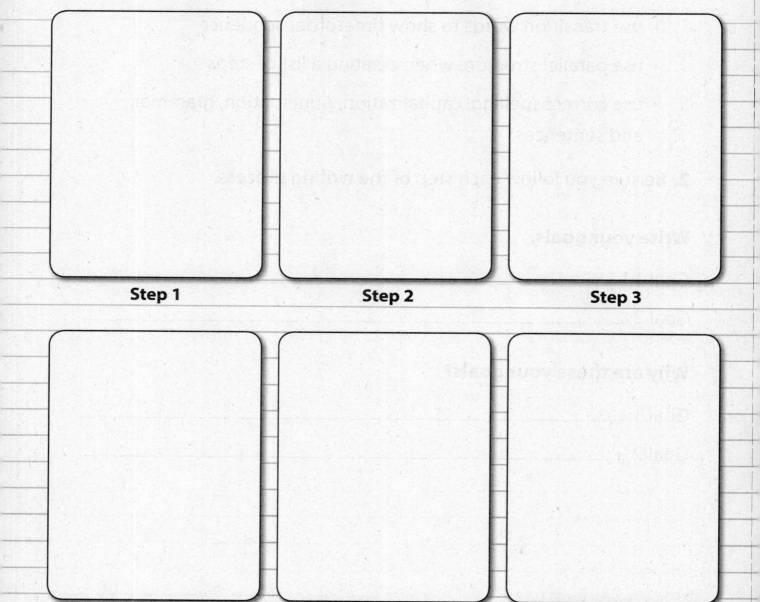

Step 1   **Step 2**   **Step 3**

Step 4   **Step 5**   **Step 6**

Name _____

Procedural Text

Title: <u>How to Make Taco Salad</u>

    <u>Helping Grandma in the kitchen is fun! One thing I like to help her make is taco salad. First, I tear up the lettuce into a big bowl. Second, I add meat that Grandma cooked. Third, I put canned beans on the lettuce. Next, I grate cheese and sprinkle it over the meat. Then, I add tomatoes that Grandma sliced. Next, I stir the dressing and drizzle it on the salad. Last, I crunch up tortilla chips over the top.</u>

$\rightarrow$

Name _____

Procedural Text (continued)

1. Tear up lettuce into a big bowl.
2. Add cooked meat.
3. Put beans on the lettuce.
4. Grate cheese and sprinkle it over the meat.
5. Add sliced tomatoes.
6. Stir dressing and drizzle over salad.
7. Crunch tortilla chips over the top.

Name _____

Conferencing

Based on your classmates' feedback, circle **YES** if the answer to the question is yes. Circle **NO** if you still need to work on that element.

Do I need more information? If yes, add words, phrases, or sentences to explain ideas better.	**YES NO**
Do I have information that does not support the central idea? If yes, delete words, phrases, or sentences that are not needed.	**YES NO**
Are my ideas clear? If no, rearrange words, phrases, and sentences so my readers can understand what I am saying.	**YES NO**
Are my steps in correct time order? If no, put them in time order.	**YES NO**
Do my steps give all the information the reader needs? If no, add the missing information.	**YES NO**

How will you fix it?

Pick one item in your writing that you want to improve. Explain how you will improve it.

_____

_____

Proofreading

Proofreading a Procedural Text Written by

_____

Editors Write your name next to the item you are checking.
Circle **YES** if the answer is yes. Circle **NO** if the answer is no.

Editor's Name	Question		
	Does the paper have the writer's name?	YES	NO
	Does the first word in each sentence start with a capital letter?	YES	NO
	Does each sentence have an action verb?	YES	NO
	Are time-order words used correctly and followed by a comma?	YES	NO
	Does each sentence use end punctuation correctly?	YES	NO
	Are words spelled correctly?	YES	NO

Writers Use this feedback to make edits to your draft. As you write
your final copy, practice joining the cursive letters together.

Name _____

Are You Ready to Publish?

Place a check mark next to the question if you can answer yes.

☑

☐	Does your text have a title?
☐	Is your name on the paper?
☐	Is your writing neat and easy to read?
☐	Does your final copy include all your previous edits and revisions?
☐	Is your writing free of errors?
☐	Did you form your cursive letters correctly?
☐	Did you connect the letters in each word?

Write two ideas for ways to make your published text better.

1. _____

_____

2. _____

_____

Name _____

Published! My How-To Paragraph

Title: _____

Author: _____

_____

_____

_____

_____

_____

_____

_____

_____

_____

As you write, remember to form your cursive letters correctly and to connect letters in each word.

Name _____

Published! My How-To List

Title: _____

Author: _____

_____

_____

_____

_____

_____

_____

_____

_____

_____

As you write, remember to form your cursive letters correctly and to connect letters in each word.

Name _____

Revisit Your Writing Goals

How Did I Do? Think about your procedural text. Place a check mark next to each goal you met.

- [ ] I stated my topic clearly.

- [ ] I used primary and secondary sources to answer my questions.

- [ ] I used transition words to show time order.

- [ ] I used parallel structure in my list of steps.

- [ ] I edited my writing for errors in spelling.

- [ ] I edited my writing for errors in capitalization and punctuation.

Did you meet other goals? Add them here.

- [ ] _____

- [ ] _____

Name _____

Cite Sources: An Example

What is the source?

Type: Book

Title: A–Z Amazing Animals of the Amazon Rainforest

Author: Mindy Sawyer

Date: 2017

How do you cite it?

Sawyer, Mindy. A–Z Amazing Animals of the Amazon Rainforest. 2017.

Your Turn! Cite this source on the lines below.

Type: Book

Title: Elephants

Author: Arthur Barrett

Date: 2015

_____ _____ _____

Fact Sheet

Pick one animal from the story. Write its name on the line. Write facts from the story about the animal. Write the page number where you found the fact.

Animal: _____

Fact 1: p. _____

_____

_____

Fact 2: p. _____

_____

_____

Source: Cherry, Lynne. <u>The Great Kapok Tree</u>. 1990.

Is this a **primary** or a **secondary** source? Circle one.

Primary | Secondary

Use the facts to answer this question:

Why is the Great Kapok Tree important to this animal?

_____

_____

_____

Name _____

Word Bank

Add interesting words or words that are new to you. Refer to these words when you begin drafting your research report.

My Research Plan

As you write your research report, be sure to:

• develop and follow a research plan

• state your central idea clearly

• ask research questions

• identify and find sources to answer your questions

• find information to answer your questions

• state facts in your own words and cite sources

Get Started! Write your research topic and plan here.

_____

_____

_____

_____

_____

_____

_____

_____

Name _____

Animal Relationships

Think of animals that have relationships with another living thing, such as a plant, another animal, or people. Your teacher will model one or two examples for you.

Animal	Relationship	Living Thing
frogs	live in	trees

1. Star one animal relationship in the chart you would like to know more about.

2. Write one research question you have about that animal relationship.

_____

_____

Name _____

My Idea Map

Write your ideas about your animal. Then write questions you have about the animal.

My Animal: _____

What I Know: _____

_____

_____

_____

What I Want to Know: _____

_____

_____

_____

Question 1: _____

_____

Question 2: _____

_____

Question 3: _____

_____

Name _____

Set Goals for Writing

1. Be sure your research report includes:

   - an introduction with a clear lead sentence with your topic

   - a body with facts that answer your research questions

   - facts that are stated in your own words

   - a conclusion that summarizes your topic

   - a list of sources that are cited properly

   - correct spelling, capitalization, and punctuation

2. Be sure you follow each step of the writing process.

Write your own goals.

Goal 1: _____

Goal 2: _____

Why are these your goals?

Goal 1: _____

Goal 2: _____

My Research Notes

Use one form for each fact. Write the fact in your own words.

My Research Question

_____

_____

My Fact

_____

_____

My Source

Circle the source type. Then fill in the information to cite the source.

Book | Magazine | Website | Person | Other: _____

Source Type: Primary | Secondary

Title: _____

Author: _____

Date: _____

Citation: _____

_____

Name _____

Research Report

Title: <u>Elephants Help Others</u>

   Elephants are very helpful and caring animals. The adults take care of the babies. All of the elephants in a herd help protect each other and defend against enemies. Elephants show that they care about each other. They can tell when another elephant is scared. They pat or stroke the scared elephant with their trunks.

   Elephants help other animals. They use their strong tusks to dig for water under the ground. In this way, they make water holes that other animals can use.

(→)

Research Report (continued)

Elephants also help people. People train them to carry loads. Elephants provide transportation for people, too.

   Elephants show they care about others by helping other elephants, other animals, and even people.

Sources

Foote, Sandra. Interview with a Zookeeper. September 2017.

Miller, Dana. "Elephants in the Wild." Big Animals Magazine, June 2017: 9–10.

Walker, Amara. Fun Facts About Elephants. 2015.

Name _____

My Report – Getting Started

Use your notes to start organizing your report.

Introduction

Body

Conclusion

Sources

Name _____

Conferencing

Based on your classmates' feedback, circle **YES** if the answer to the question is yes. Circle **NO** if you still need to work on that element.

Do I need more information? If yes, add words, phrases, or sentences to explain ideas better.	YES	NO
Do I have information that does not support the central idea? If yes, delete words, phrases, or sentences that are not needed.	YES	NO
Are my ideas clear? If no, rearrange words, phrases, and sentences so your readers can understand what you are saying.	YES	NO
Does the introduction state the topic clearly?	YES	NO
Does the conclusion summarize the topic?	YES	NO

How will you fix it?

Pick one item in your writing that you want to improve. Explain how you will improve it.

_____

_____

Proofreading

Proofreading a Research Report Written by

_____

Editors Write your name next to the item you are checking.
Circle **YES** if the answer is yes. Circle **NO** if the answer is no.

Editor's Name	Question		
	Does the paper have the writer's name?	YES	NO
	Do sentences start with a capital letter?	YES	NO
	Do the subject and verb agree in number?	YES	NO
	Is a conjunction used in a compound subject?	YES	NO
	Is a conjunction used in a compound predicate?	YES	NO
	Does each sentence use end punctuation correctly?	YES	NO

Writers Use this feedback to edit your research report. As you write,
be sure to join the cursive letters correctly.

Name _____

Published!

Publish your research report here or on a separate sheet of paper. Write in cursive. Focus on how you join the letters in each word. Add interesting details to grab your reader's attention, such as a drawing.

Name _____

Revisit Your Writing Goals

How Did I Do? Congratulations! You finished your research report. Review the writing goals you set earlier for writing a research report. Did you meet your goals? What could you do better with your next piece of writing? Write two or three sentences that tell how you think you did.

_____

_____

_____

_____

_____

_____

_____

_____

_____

_____

Name _____

Word Bank

Add words that tell about culture.

Write About Culture

Use one or two words from the box to tell about a cultural experience.

_____

_____

Name _____

Culture Web

Write words that help you understand more about a culture.

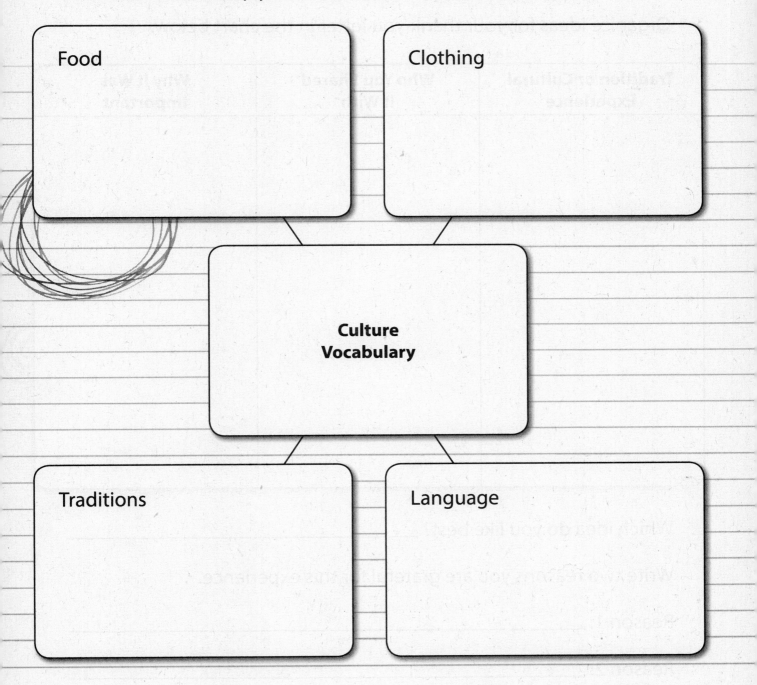

Food

Clothing

Culture Vocabulary

Traditions

Language

Your Culture Web You can create a culture web like this one for any culture.

Name _____

My Traditions and Cultural Experiences

Organize ideas for your thank-you letter in the chart below.

Tradition or Cultural Experience	Who You Shared It With	Why It Was Important

Which idea do you like best? _____

Write two reasons you are grateful for this experience.

Reason 1: _____

Reason 2: _____

Name _____

Set Goals for Writing

1. When you write your thank-you letter, be sure you:

- write a heading with the date

- write a greeting, such as *Dear Grandma*

- write a clear reason for writing the letter

- write about the experience, what you learned, and why it is important to you

- use correct spelling, capitalization, and punctuation

- write a closing and your signature

2. Be sure you follow each step of the writing process.

Write your own goals.

Goal 1: _____

Goal 2: _____

Why are these your goals?

Goal 1: _____

Goal 2: _____

Name _____

Thank-You Letter

November 4, 2019

Dear Grandpa,

Do you remember when we celebrated Chinese New Year together? I do! At first, I was afraid because there were so many people. But, you held my hand and made me feel safe.

I loved the colorful costumes in the parade, and the dragon dance was amazing. The fireworks were my favorite part. They lit up the sky with beautiful colors.

Name _____

Thank-You Letter (continued)

    Thank you for sharing this day with me. It has special meaning because I learned a lot about Chinese traditions.

Love,
Michelle

Parts of a Thank-You Letter

Write the parts of your thank-you letter.

Heading and Date: _____

_____

_____

Greeting: _____

```
Body:




```

Closing: _____

Signature: _____

Name _____

Conferencing

Based on your classmates' feedback, circle **YES** if the answer to the question is yes. Circle **NO** if you still need to work on that element.

Do I need more information? If yes, add words, phrases, or sentences to explain ideas better.	**YES** **NO**
Do I have information that does not support the central idea? If yes, delete words, phrases, or sentences that are not needed.	**YES** **NO**
Are my ideas clear? If no, rearrange words, phrases, and sentences so your readers can understand what you are saying.	**YES** **NO**
Does my thank-you letter have all the parts of a letter?	**YES** **NO**
Do the parts of my letter use proper formatting?	**YES** **NO**

How will you fix it?

Pick one item in your writing that you want to improve. Explain how you will improve it.

_____

_____

Pronouns

Check Writer's Notebook pages 10.5 and 10.6 for pronouns. Write each pronoun from the model in the correct column below.

Subject Pronouns	Object Pronouns	Possessive Pronouns
Example: we	Example: it	Example: my

Check your draft for pronouns. Write each pronoun from your draft in the correct column.

Subject Pronouns	Object Pronouns	Possessive Pronouns

Now, reread your draft. Add more pronouns as needed to help make your thank-you letter stronger.

Name _____

Proofreading

Proofreading a Thank-You Letter Written by

_____

Editors Write your name next to the item you are checking.

Circle **YES** if the answer is yes. Circle **NO** if the answer is no.

Editor's Name	Question		
	Is the pronoun "I" capitalized?	YES	NO
	Are proper nouns capitalized?	YES	NO
	Are commas used in a series?	YES	NO
	Is a comma used in the greeting?	YES	NO
	Is a comma used in the closing?	YES	NO
	Does the letter end with the writer's signature?	YES	NO

Writers Use this feedback to edit your draft. Connect the letters in each word together in cursive handwriting. Be sure the lines are not too short or too long.

Name _____

Revisit Your Writing Goals

How Did I Do? Place a check mark in the column that shows how you did. Then complete the sentence frames below.

Did I meet this goal?	Yes	No	Almost
I wrote a heading with the date.			
I wrote a greeting correctly.			
The body included a clear reason for writing the letter.			
The body included the experience and why it was important to me.			
I wrote a closing and signature.			
I used correct spelling.			
I used correct punctuation.			

The best thing about my letter was _____ .

Next time, I would like to improve _____

_____ .

Share Your Writing

Make a check mark in the box if the answer is yes.

When your partner shared the thank-you letter, did your partner:

☐	read in a loud, clear voice?
☐	read with expression?
☐	group phrases for meaning?
☐	use punctuation to know when to pause?
☐	use punctuation to know when to ask a question?
☐	use punctuation to know when to use emotion?
☐	look at the audience?

Share feedback. Give the paper to your partner. Then, talk about how your partner did. Use the sentence frames below.

When you shared your thank-you letter, you _____ .

I like how you _____ when you shared your thank-you letter.

Class Poll

Complete the chart below to tally the class's feelings about the activities.

Activity	Number of Votes for *Scary*	Number of Votes for *Exciting*
1. ride a bike		
2. read aloud to the class		
3. fly in an airplane		
4. go down a very tall water slide		
5.		
6.		

Which activity does the class think is the most scary?

_____

Which activity does the class think is the most exciting?

_____

How do you know?

_____

Word Bank

Write examples of descriptive and figurative language. You can use this Word Bank when you draft and revise your own personal narrative.

Adjectives and Adverbs	Action Verbs	Onomatopoeia

Use one or more words from the chart in a sentence.

_____

_____

Name _____

Set Goals for Writing

1. Be sure your personal narrative includes:

- a story that tells about something new you did or tried to do

- you as the person telling the story

- other characters

- a beginning, a middle, and an end

- descriptive language, including adjectives, adverbs, and action verbs

- figurative language, including onomatopoeia

2. Be sure you follow each step of the writing process.

Write your goals.

Goal 1: _____

Goal 2: _____

Why are these your goals?

Goal 1: _____

Goal 2: _____

Name _____

Ask Questions

My topic: _____

Questions a reader might ask me about my topic:

Who: _____

_____

What: _____

_____

Where: _____

_____

Why: _____

_____

When: _____

_____

How: _____

_____

Name _____

Personal Narrative

Title: <u>First-Time Bike Rider</u>

   I remember the first time I tried riding a bike. I was five years old, and I really wanted to know how because my neighbor Sani had a bike. But I was scared to try. Every time I watched Sani speed off on two wheels, I marveled at how she could even keep her balance. It seemed like a feat meant only for gymnasts.

   I was not a gymnast. In fact, I wasn't even good at patting my head while rubbing my stomach. How on earth could I ever balance and steer a bike at the same time?

Personal Narrative (continued)

Still, I *really* wanted to ride bikes with Sani. So, I asked my mom to help me learn. That Saturday, she drove me to the school parking lot.

On weekends, the school parking lot is empty. It is also wide open and flat. Mom took me there to practice. She got out my bike and held it upright.

"Climb on," she said. "I'll hold the bike." Even this simple first step made me feel nervous. But, I climbed on. Mom could see I was already starting to panic.

$\rightarrow$

Personal Narrative (continued)

"Don't worry," she said. "I'm not going to let go. I'm just going to take you for a little ride, so you can see how it feels." Mom held the bike's handlebar and seat. She rolled me forward slowly.

"Now, put your feet on the pedals," she said. I hadn't even thought about having to pedal! How was I ever going to do this? "Don't fret," she said. "Just try."

I did, and we rode around like that for a while. At first, my feet kept losing hold of the pedals. But soon, I got into a rhythm: *Pushhh* left, *pushhh* right, *pushhh* left, *pushhh* right.

$\rightarrow$

Name _____

Personal Narrative (continued)

The bike tires whispered and whirred beneath me.

Then I realized with a shock that Mom wasn't holding the bike anymore! I tottered to the side and caught myself with my left foot. My heart beat wildly.

At first, I didn't know if I was excited or miffed with my mom. But Mom was smiling and clapping joyfully. I decided I was excited.

I wish I could say the rest was easy. It took a few more practices before I was ready to ride bikes with Sani. But I was definitely glad I had tried. Now, riding a bike is one of my favorite things to do.

Story Structure

Continue to draft your personal narrative in the chart below.

Beginning
Introduce characters, a setting, and a conflict:

↓

Middle
Tell how and why your feelings changed as you faced the conflict:

↓

End
Describe the resolution and tell how it made you feel:

11.9

Name _____

Conferencing

Based on your classmates' feedback, circle **YES** if the answer to the question is yes. Circle **NO** if you still need to work on that element.

Do I need more information? If yes, add words, phrases, or sentences to explain ideas better.	YES NO
Do I have information that does not support the central idea? If yes, delete words, phrases, or sentences that are not needed.	YES NO
Are my ideas clear? If no, rearrange words, phrases, and sentences so readers can understand the ideas.	YES NO
Does my narrative have a clear beginning, middle, and end?	YES NO
Is it clear that I am the narrator of the story?	YES NO

How will you fix it?

Pick one item in your writing that you want to improve. Explain how you will improve it.

_____

_____

Proofreading

Proofreading a Personal Narrative Written by _____

Editors Write your name next to the item you are checking.
Circle **YES** if the answer is yes. Circle **NO** if the answer is no.

Editor's Name	Question		
	Is the writer's name on the paper?	YES	NO
	Are first-person pronouns used?	YES	NO
	Is the pronoun "I" capitalized?	YES	NO
	Do the subject and verb in each sentence agree?	YES	NO
	Does each sentence start with a capital letter?	YES	NO
	Does each sentence use end punctuation correctly?	YES	NO
	Are all words spelled correctly?	YES	NO

Writers Use this checklist to edit your personal narrative. Write in cursive. Focus on how you join the letters in each word.

Name _____

Revisit Your Writing Goals

How Did I Do? Congratulations! You finished your personal narrative. Look at the writing goals you set on Writer's Notebook page 11.3 or in your own notebook. Did you meet them? What could you do better with your next piece of writing? Write two or three sentences that tell how you think you did.

_____

_____

_____

_____

_____

_____

_____

_____

My Dot

Draw a dot. Add details to create a picture from your dot.

Name _____

Word Bank

Write words and phrases from the story and from your own experiences that help create a mental image.

Use words from the box in a sentence that states an opinion or that supports an opinion.

_____

_____

_____

Opinion Essay

Title: <u>Learning to Play Piano</u>

I believe that learning to play the piano is hard.

The first time I tried to play, I didn't know where to put my fingers. In the beginning, it seemed like there were just too many keys. Some are black and some are white. How could I know where to put my fingers? How would I know which keys to play? With all these questions, I knew that learning to play the piano was going to be hard!

$\longrightarrow$

Name _____

Opinion Essay (continued)

    My music teacher pointed to the music as I pressed the keys. Later, he helped me see that the white and black keys are set in a pattern. He told me that knowing this pattern would help me learn to play the piano.

    In addition, my teacher said practicing each day would help me know which keys to use. I knew I would not learn to play piano overnight. I would have to stick with it and keep practicing.

    As I practiced, it was frustrating to hit the wrong keys and make awful sounds. But I kept trying.

→

Name _____

Opinion Essay (continued)

For a while, it didn't sound so great. After much practice, the notes I pressed began to sound like a song. I kept practicing because I believed in myself. I believed I could learn how to play the piano. Now, I can play many songs on the piano. I enjoy playing new songs for my family and friends.

    In summary, learning to play the piano taught me to stick with a task, believe in myself, and appreciate the joy of learning something new. In my opinion, learning to play the piano is hard, but it's a good skill to learn.

Name _____

Set Goals for Writing

1. Be sure your opinion essay includes:

    • your opinion statement

    • support for your opinion such as facts, figures, and examples

    • topic-specific words and linking words to create a strong, engaging message

    • a conclusion that summarizes your opinion

    • correct spelling, capitalization, punctuation, and grammar

2. Be sure you follow each step of the writing process.

Write your goals.

Goal 1: _____

Goal 2: _____

Why are these your goals?

Goal 1: _____

Goal 2: _____

Support Your Opinion

Use this page to draft the elements of your opinion essay.

Introduction

State your opinion:

Body

Reason 1:

Reason 2:

Reason 3:

Conclusion

State your conclusion and convince your audience:

Name _____

Conferencing

Use this checklist to check your opinion essay based on your group's feedback.

Do I need more information? If yes, add words, phrases, or sentences to explain ideas better.	YES NO
Do I have information that does not support the central idea? If yes, delete words, phrases, or sentences that are not needed.	YES NO
Are my ideas clear? If no, rearrange words, phrases, and sentences so readers can understand the ideas.	YES NO
Is my opinion stated clearly? If no, use the feedback to revise the opinion statement.	YES NO
Do my reasons support my opinion? If no, use the feedback to provide stronger reasons.	YES NO

How will you fix it?

Pick one item in your writing that you want to improve. Explain how you will improve it.

_____

_____

Proofreading

Proofreading an Opinion Essay Written by _____

Editors Write your name next to the item you are checking.
Circle **YES** if the answer is yes. Circle **NO** if the answer is no.

Editor's Name	Question		
	Does the paper have the writer's name?	YES	NO
	Does each sentence start with a capital letter?	YES	NO
	Does each sentence have subject-verb agreement?	YES	NO
	Does each sentence use the correct verb tense?	YES	NO
	Did the writer use time/place adverbs correctly?	YES	NO
	Is end punctuation used correctly?	YES	NO
	Are words spelled correctly?	YES	NO

Writers Use this feedback to edit your draft. As you write, remember
to join the cursive letters correctly.

Name _____

Revisit Your Writing Goals

How Did I Do? Congratulations! You finished your opinion essay. Look at the goals you set on Writer's Notebook page 12.6 or in your notebook. Did you meet them? What could you do better with your next piece of writing? Write two or three sentences that tell how you think you did.

_____

_____

_____

_____

_____

_____

_____

_____

_____